MARKET EMINENCE

MARKET EMINENCE

**22 Strategies to Build a
Bold Personal Brand,
Become a Business Celebrity,
and Drive Unstoppable Growth**

DAVID NEWMAN, CSP

Copyright © 2026 by David Newman

All rights reserved. No part of this book may be reproduced, stored in a retrieval system or transmitted, in any form or by any means, without the prior written consent of the publisher, except in the case of brief quotations, embodied in reviews and articles.

Cataloguing in publication information is available from Library and Archives Canada.

ISBN 978-1-77458-746-1 (paperback)
ISBN 978-1-77458-747-8 (ebook)

Page Two
pagetwo.com

Page Two™ is a trademark owned by
Page Two Strategies Inc., and is used under
license by authorized licensees

www.marketeminence.com

The book you hold in your hands is the ultimate playbook to **escape best-kept-secret syndrome, grow your company exponentially,** and **earn the visibility, credibility, and brand preference that you deserve**. To make the experience even more valuable, I've compiled all the free companion tools, resources, worksheets, and bonus trainings at:

www.marketeminence.com

Go get them now!

CONTENTS

Introduction 1

How to Use This Book 4

PART 1 **SETTING THE STAGE FOR MARKET EMINENCE** 9

PART 2 **THE MARKET EMINENCE PLAYBOOK** 31

    1 Influence: The Currency of Market Leaders 40

    2 Slant: Profitable Polarization 46

    3 Future: Your Vision That Leads 52

    4 Meaning: Unlock Deeper Connections 58

    5 Thinking: Own the Ideas That Matter 64

    6 Resistance: Fight What's Worth Fighting For 70

    7 Gifts: Love Them in Advance 76

    8 Certainty: Conviction That Converts 82

    9 Gravity: Become a Market Magnet 88

   10 Risks: Smart Bets That Pay Off 94

11 **Myths: Challenge the BS** 100

12 **Friends: The Company Your Brand Keeps** 106

13 **Lens: Your Signature Way of Seeing** 112

14 **Manifesto: Your Bold Declaration** 118

15 **Mantras: Your Quotability Quotient** 124

16 **Breakage: Strategic Reinvention** 132

17 **Language: Words That Set You Apart** 138

18 **Legends: Stories Worth Retelling** 144

19 **Friction: To Protect and to Serve** 150

20 **Momentum: Become an Unstoppable Force** 156

21 **Speed: Move Fast and Keep Moving** 162

PART 3 MARKET EMINENCE IN ACTION 169

22 **The Market Eminence Model** 170

Conclusion 178

If you're excited to grow your company and become more in demand because of who you are and how you see the world, you're in the right place.

INTRODUCTION

Why market eminence, and why now?

Because your personal brand isn't something you can safely ignore anymore. In a world drowning in noise, the worst thing you can be is forgettable.

Look around. Your field has plenty of smart, capable, hardworking leaders, but not many **truly stand out**.

Even fewer have earned **genuine trust**.

And just a handful reach **market eminence**: that special place where their words carry real weight, their name becomes the brand, and their business grows like crazy because of who they are and how they show up.

The word "eminence" means distinction or recognized superiority, especially within a particular sphere or profession.

Synonyms include renown, greatness, prestige, importance, reputation, fame, celebrity, prominence, and status.

That's what this book will help you create, whether you're a founder, expert, or professional services leader.

Until now most advice on personal branding has been too fluffy, gotten lost in tactics, or focused too much on surface looks rather than real substance.

This book changes that.

You'll get 22 deep-dive strategies to build a strong personal brand, become known for your bold ideas, and drive serious growth.

You'll become the trusted face of your firm, the respected voice in your field, and the magnet that pulls in perfect-fit clients, partners, talent, investors, and media without chasing, convincing, or begging them.

Each short chapter will spark new thinking and brave choices and show you easy ways to apply these ideas to your exact situation and goals.

Listen, you don't need to be famous. But you **do** need to be known, trusted, and remembered by the people who matter most.

I'm here to help you:

- **Build** a standout personal brand that drives real business growth.
- **Link** your personal visibility to your company's market position.
- **Turn** bold, different thinking into more revenue, recognition, and respect.
- **Become** impossible to ignore in your industry and impossible to replace.

This book guides you to find your voice and build a brand that outlasts trends, withstands economic downturns, and beats competitors regardless of external conditions.

If you're ready to create business momentum that will last for years to come, this book is for you.

Your market eminence starts now.

DAVID NEWMAN
Bryn Mawr, PA

HOW TO USE THIS BOOK

Whether you've read any of my three other books (*Do It! Marketing*, *Do It! Speaking*, and *Do It! Selling*) or not, we need to get something straight right from the start.

This book is different. It's shorter, tighter, leaner, and meaner.

But most importantly...
This is **not** a how-to book.
It's much more valuable than that.

This is a how-to-think book.

> **NOTE**
>
> Throughout this book you'll find free companion tools, resources, and training that you can download, print, and share with your team by visiting:
> **www.marketeminence.com**

Because personal branding (real, results-producing, market-dominating branding) isn't gimmicks, cool logos, or ego-driven hype.

It's the mental frameworks, strategic shifts, and leadership-level decisions that elevate you and your firm from being just another name in a crowded market to being the brand that **leads**.

Even smart, insightful CEOs, founders, and experts whose firms do great work, forge innovative ideas, and deliver amazing results, still struggle with:

- **Chasing clients**, investors, and partners, constantly pitching instead of being pursued.
- **Blending in** with look-alike competitors, with no clear reason why your name should rise to the top.
- **Being overlooked** by decision-makers, industry media, and influential partners who give their attention to better known (but less qualified) voices.
- **Relying on referrals** and word of mouth as your primary (and unpredictable) growth engine.
- **Having a reputation** that doesn't reflect the scale of your accomplishments or the ambition of your vision.
- **Burning time**, energy, and patience on long, slow sales cycles because prospects don't know who you are.
- **Getting passed over** for high-visibility opportunities like keynotes, panels, and podcast interviews.

In Part 1 of the book, you'll get rocket fuel in the form of provocations, observations, and insights into why your market eminence matters now more than ever.

Then in Part 2, you'll blast off into the stratosphere of market eminence, where only the top 5 percent of elite founders, entrepreneurs, and experts operate. This is the truly exciting part, because when you achieve market eminence, you will:

- **Attract top-tier clients, partners, and investors** who now proactively seek you out, not vice versa.
- **Own your niche** and become the definitive voice in your industry.
- **Command attention and respect** from media, peers, and competitors alike.
- **Build a platform that scales your influence** far beyond word of mouth or referrals.
- **Turn your reputation into a magnet** for high-value opportunities.
- **Shortcut sales cycles** because prospects show up already sold on you.
- **Get invited to the right rooms, stages, and deals** because you're seen as essential.

- **Future-proof your business** by becoming AI-proof, price-proof, and competition-proof.
- **Create lasting strategic advantage** that no one else can duplicate.
- **Lead a movement, not just a company,** and amplify your long-term impact.

By deeply working through each of the following 22 strategies, you'll redefine how you see yourself, your business, your audience, and your role as the face of a market-dominating brand.

If you're looking for tactics, you'll find them in Part 3, but only in service of a bigger mission:

Your rise to lasting market eminence.

If you're ready to stop playing small, stop blending in, and finally build the brand your business (and your future) deserves...

Let's go.

SETTING THE STAGE FOR MARKET EMINENCE

PART ONE

THE AWAKENING

There comes a moment when everything changes.

It might happen while reading a book like this one.

Or during a talk with a mentor, or in the middle of the night.

It's that moment when you can no longer deny what you've always known: You were meant for more.

This awakening isn't ego or ambition. It's purpose. It's finally recognizing that your unique combination of skills, experiences, and perspective isn't random. It's a tool kit precisely calibrated for the contribution only you can make.

When this hits you, your doubts and fears don't completely go away, but a clearer, stronger voice joins in: the voice of certainty. The voice that says, "This is where I belong. This is the difference I'm meant to make."

And suddenly, the way forward no longer means competing with others or following their well-worn paths. You start expressing your conviction so powerfully that it creates its own category.

There's nothing stopping you and nothing to wait for. **This can happen right now.** Not when you get more degrees, not when you have more followers, and not when someone gives you permission.

It's today, exactly as you are, with exactly what you have.

Your market eminence journey begins with this single, powerful recognition: You're already the authority.

Now it's time to act like it.

THE INVISIBLE ENEMY

Every morning, you wake up with a choice. Will today be the day you finally show everyone how good you really are?

Or will you try to fit in, not draw attention, and stay in the background?

I've watched brilliant minds settle for mediocrity. I've seen world-class expertise remain hidden in the shadows. I've witnessed revolutionary ideas go nowhere because the person who conceived them didn't believe they had the right to share them boldly.

This is a form of betrayal. Not just of yourself, but of those who need what only you can provide.

That voice in your head saying, "Who do you think you are to stand out?" isn't being wise or humble. It's fear pretending to be caution.

It's the invisible force that keeps your business smaller than it should be, your impact narrower than it could be, your voice quieter than it needs to be.

See this negative force for what it is. Then decide once and for all, starting today, that you won't give in to it anymore.

The world doesn't reward people who hide their talents.

The marketplace doesn't notice people who whisper.

THE OBSCURITY TAX

You're paying it every day. You might not see the line item on your profit-and-loss statement, but it's the heaviest tax your business bears: the obscurity tax.

It's the premium clients who go elsewhere because your brand lacks conviction. The top talent that never considers working for you. The media opportunities that flow to your more distinctive competitors. The partnerships that never materialize because you're invisible.

This isn't occasional revenue leakage. It's a constant, massive hemorrhage of opportunity.

And you've accepted it. You've normalized it. You've convinced yourself that "this is just how my industry works" or "we're doing as well as can be expected." This comfortable lie lets you avoid confronting the brutal truth: Your unwillingness to get seen and stand out is costing you everything.

The obscurity tax isn't imposed by some external authority. You volunteer to pay it every time you dilute your message to avoid offending anyone.

Every time you copy competitors instead of charting your own course.

Every time you choose safe and forgettable over bold and memorable.

This tax isn't inevitable. It's a choice.

And you can stop paying it right now.

THE BORROWED VOICE

If you're like most people we work with, here's the first thing we need to fix: You don't sound like *you*.

You sound just like everyone else.

Your website text reads like it was written by the same person who wrote your competitor's. Your social media articles blend right in with all the similar articles in your field. Your presentations use the same old structure with the same tired phrases.

Somewhere along the way, you started thinking that sounding professional equals sounding boring. That sharing your expertise requires buzzwords and jargon.

That being respected means sounding like everyone else with their fancy credentials or awards.

This isn't just bad branding. It's intellectual cowardice because it shows you're afraid to be yourself. So, you adopted a borrowed voice. That sanitized, homogenized, soul-sucking approximation of what you think an authority in your field should sound like.

And in doing so, you surrendered the one thing the market craves: your authentic perspective delivered in your genuine voice.

If you can't tell the difference between your content and your competitor's when the logos are removed, you don't have a brand. You have camouflage.

Stop hiding. Stop copying. Stop being so afraid of sounding like yourself.

Your borrowed voice isn't fooling anyone... except maybe you.

THE SOFT ADDICTION

We're drawn to what's comfortable, not what's necessary.

Look at your calendar. Look at your inbox. Look at how you spent your time yesterday. How much of it was devoted to activities that will elevate your brand to market eminence? And how much of it was lost to the soft addiction of busywork?

Most leaders are hooked on distractions that feel productive: checking email 60 times a day, sitting in meetings that should have been emails, tweaking website copy that's already good enough, responding to the urgent at the expense of the important.

This is what avoidance looks like.

The tasks that would truly elevate your brand are precisely the ones most likely to trigger discomfort: The bold stance that might alienate some to deeply connect with others. The speaking opportunity that requires you to own your expertise in the limelight. The premium pricing model that repels transactional buyers while attracting great clients who are fully committed to getting great results.

So instead, you reach for another tiny hit of comfortable productivity. Another email answered. Another report reviewed. Another minor task completed.

Meanwhile, your position in the market stays exactly the same. Your competitors keep playing it safe too.

But here's the good news:

The escape hatch is wide open for anyone with the courage to step through it.

THE EXPERTISE DELUSION

You think you're not getting the recognition you deserve because people don't understand how good you are.

This comforting delusion lets you blame the market's ignorance rather than help you confront the real problem.

The harsh truth is the market doesn't reward expertise. It rewards the *perception* of expertise.

And the perception isn't created by your credentials, your experience, or even your results. It's created by your ability to articulate your distinct point of view with absolute clarity and conviction.

There are thousands of founders, entrepreneurs, and experts in your field with impressive skills who remain completely unknown.

Meanwhile, others with half their knowledge command authority, attract clients, and shape the conversation.

Infuriating and unfair, isn't it? The difference isn't knowledge. It's courage.

The courage to stake a clear position. To challenge conventional thinking. To say "This is what I believe" instead of hedging, hesitating, and hand-wringing.

Your expertise becomes valuable only when it's expressed fully and freely.

Your knowledge matters only when it's applied to a point of view.

And your experience counts only when it shapes a perspective that others can understand, repeat, and remember.

THE FALSE ABUNDANCE ABUNDANCE ABUNDANCE

There's never been more content, more experts, more information.

And yet there's never been less true wisdom, less genuine authority, less meaningful perspective.

This paradox creates your opportunity. In a world drowning in how-to content generated by AI, recycled by amateurs, and pumped into feeds by the terabyte, depth has become the rarest commodity of all.

The market doesn't need another "thought leader" sharing platitudes. It doesn't need another "expert" repeating what everyone else is saying. It's suffocating under the weight of all this sameness masquerading as insight.

What the market desperately needs is someone with the courage to think deeply, speak truthfully, and stand firmly on ground they've personally explored.

Someone whose perspective comes from lived experience, not borrowed authority. Someone whose voice cuts through the noise precisely because it isn't trying to appeal to everyone.

This is the new scarcity:
- Not information, but **interpretation**.
- Not content, but **conviction**.
- Not visibility, but **vision**.

The leaders who emerge in this environment won't be those who speak the loudest or publish the most.

They'll be those who say something worth hearing in the first place.

THE GENEROSITY PARADOX

How many times have you heard the old internet marketing trick "Give them the What but don't give them the How," as if withholding it will force prospects to hire you?

Those gurus recommend you keep your best ideas hidden, charge big money for your insights, and never reveal how you do what you do.

The counterintuitive path to market eminence runs in the opposite direction: toward radical generosity.

Toward giving away insights that others charge for. Toward teaching what you know rather than teasing with what you might reveal.

This isn't just being nice. It's being smart. When you share your best thinking freely, you show real confidence, build lasting trust, and attract people who genuinely want to hear from you.

The leaders who achieve market eminence aren't stingy with their knowledge because they understand that the value isn't in what you know; it's in how you apply what you know to specific situations that matter.

Your generosity doesn't diminish your value; it proves it. Your openness doesn't reduce demand; it increases it.

Be radically helpful. Be radically generous.

The more you share, the more people will recognize the depth of your expertise and respect the distinctive way you see the world.

THE VALUATION $ECRET

The most common question from the CEOs and experts I work with is "If I become the face of my brand, how can I ever sell the company?"

This fear keeps countless founders hiding in the shadows. It seems logical: Make yourself replaceable from day one.

But that's not how valuable businesses are built.

Look at the evidence. HubSpot's Brian Halligan and Dharmesh Shah remained highly visible throughout their company's growth to a $37.7-billion valuation.

ExactTarget's Scott Dorsey was the recognized face of his email marketing firm when Salesforce acquired it for $2.5 billion.

Constant Contact's Gail Goodman built her personal brand alongside her company's, leading to a $1.1-billion acquisition by Endurance International Group.

Acquirers don't want anonymous businesses. They want category leaders with distinctive market positions. That rarely happens without a founder brave enough to be visible.

Maximum valuation doesn't come from founders retreating into obscurity. The key is to amplify your leadership voice to establish market dominance while simultaneously building systems, teams, and intellectual property that can eventually operate without you.

Don't diminish your firm's value out of fear.

The most sellable businesses are those whose founders use their personal brand (writing articles, speaking at conferences, appearing on podcasts, publishing books) to create unmistakable market eminence.

THE CROSSROAD

Once you've reached the end of this book, you'll have a choice.

Will you **continue** as you were before? Merely competent, respectable, unremarkable?

Or will you **commit** to the path of market eminence and become the leader who shapes conversations, attracts opportunities, and builds a legacy that extends far beyond business results?

This isn't just a philosophical question. It's a practical one with **real consequences** for your business, your team, your future, and the people you serve.

The world doesn't need more businesses that blend in. It doesn't need more leaders who play it safe.

What it desperately needs are voices of clarity and conviction. Leaders who stand for something meaningful. Experts who share their best thinking without fear.

The path to market eminence isn't easy. It requires courage, consistency, and a willingness to be deeply, authentically seen. It means choosing substance over surface, long-term impact over short-term comfort, and meaningful distinction over safe similarity.

But for those who choose this path, the rewards are extraordinary. Not just in business growth and market position, but in the profound satisfaction of knowing you've fully expressed your unique contribution.

The choice is yours. What will you decide?

PART TWO

THE MARKET EMINENCE PLAYBOOK

Before we dive into the 22 strategies that will drive your market eminence, let's start with a quick diagnostic.

The following self-assessment will help you pinpoint exactly where you are on the spectrum from market obscurity to market eminence.

YOUR MARKET EMINENCE SCORECARD

For each statement below, rate yourself from 1 to 5:

1. Strongly Disagree
2. Disagree
3. Neutral / Not Sure
4. Agree
5. Strongly Agree

CLARITY + DIFFERENTIATION

I can clearly articulate what makes me different from others in my industry. _____

I have a bold, contrarian point of view that I publicly share. _____

I've defined a unique lens or framework for how I see my target market and their problems. _____

I reject common industry practices and say so loud and proud. _____

My audience knows not just what I do but what I stand for and stand against. _____

SUBTOTAL _____

VISIBILITY + INFLUENCE

I'm consistently visible on key platforms where my audience hangs out. _____

I speak regularly (in person and virtually) to targeted audiences. _____

I publish sharply differentiated and opinionated content that drives new leads. _____

I'm frequently invited to appear on key podcasts, webinars, or panels in my target market. _____

My voice is seen as credible and authoritative by peers and decision-makers. _____

SUBTOTAL _____

TRUST + GRAVITAS

I have proof (case studies, metrics, testimonials) to back up my claims of client results. _____

My brand feels magnetic; I consistently attract the right clients, partners, investors, and talent. _____

People often say they feel like I "can read their mind" or "totally get them." _____

I show up consistently with a distinctive and easily recognizable tone, voice, and character. _____

My pricing reflects my brand's premium positioning and high-value results. _____

SUBTOTAL _____

MOMENTUM + EXPANSION

I maintain a steady cadence of content, engagement, and brand presence with my target market. _____

I've turned my brand into an ecosystem with reliable partners, referral sources, and a client community. _____

I've created strategic alliances with like-minded companies to expand into new niches or verticals. _____

My brand has staying power; it's not dependent on any one channel, market, trend, or tactic. _____

I've built a team or system to sustain ongoing brand activity without burning out. _____

SUBTOTAL _____

YOUR SCORE

Add your subtotals

Clarity + Differentiation	_____ / 25
Visibility + Influence	_____ / 25
Trust + Gravitas	_____ / 25
Momentum + Expansion	_____ / 25
TOTAL SCORE	_____ **/100**

WHAT YOUR SCORE MEANS

85–100: Market eminence status
You're already a force in your industry, but there's still room to push the envelope and scale your impact. Time to amplify and expand.

65–84: Strong foundation
You've got the bones of market eminence, so let's add muscle. Tighten your brand, sharpen your slant, and dial up your visibility.

45–64: Rising star
You're building momentum, but a few key strategic shifts will help you break through the noise. Start with clarity, proof, and presence.

Under 45: Hidden gem
You've got the goods. Now it's time to stop being the best-kept secret and create the brand your market can't ignore.

Now that you know where you stand, let's roll up our sleeves and start building your market eminence.

1 INFLUENCE

THE CURRENCY OF MARKET LEADERS

QUICK DEFINITION

Every personal and company brand is shaped by external influences (culture, competitors, trends, and market conditions), but the strongest industry leaders are themselves an influential force.

HOW TO THINK

Just following trends won't cut it. The brands people remember don't just join conversations. They create them. Your ideas can change how people think about your entire industry.

Identify the trends impacting your industry
- Talk often with clients about their challenges.
- Watch what competitors are doing (and not doing).
- Set a monthly reminder to identify and reflect on the biggest changes affecting your target market. (Hint: Use Google, fresh industry data, and your favorite AI tools to discover, verify, analyze, and document your findings, then brainstorm on them.)

Choose where to apply your influence
- Not every topic deserves your attention, so be selective.
- Push your big ideas, but call out hype too.
- Skip what doesn't matter to your audience.

Shape industry conversations
- Share clear opinions that people can easily understand and remember.
- Use current events and pop culture references, analogies, and examples to make complex topics simpler.
- Package your insights so that others want to share them (simple frameworks, visual images, catchy phrases).

MIND SPARK QUESTIONS

What are our clients secretly worried about (but rarely mention) when using our products/services?

If tough regulations hit our industry tomorrow, in which areas would we be most vulnerable?

In what ways could I start pushing back on the industry hype and share ideas that simplify complexity?

Creating content about: _____

Speaking at: _____

Partnering with: _____

What are the key points I want to drive home on this issue that clients could truly benefit from?

EXERCISE
THE BRAND INFLUENCE TRACKER

List the changes. Write down three important shifts happening in your target market right now. Example: "More customers want sustainable products."

Pick your position. For each change, decide:
- "I'll embrace this" (it fits your strengths).
- "I'll challenge this" (you see a different path).
- "I'll offer a fresh perspective" (you have a unique angle).

Take action. For each position, plan one concrete step:
- Create something helpful (article, checklist, simple guide).
- Choose where to share it (LinkedIn, industry event, customer email).
- Set a date to do it in the next 30 days.

True influence isn't being the loudest. It's saying something worth repeating.

2 SLANT

PROFITABLE POLARIZATION

QUICK DEFINITION

Your slant is your unique viewpoint that makes people stop, notice, and pay attention. It's what you say differently when everyone else sounds the same. A strong slant is a key ingredient of market eminence and fuels business growth.

HOW TO THINK

When most messages blend into the bland, having a clear slant that challenges the status quo helps you stand out. When you say something different in a meaningful way, people remember you and seek you out. As a bonus, you get to have more fun, speak your mind, and help your clients all at the same time.

Define your contrarian slant
- What industry "truth" do most people accept that you disagree with?
- What approach do you take that goes against common practice?
- What problem do you solve in a way others don't, can't, or are afraid to?

Say it everywhere
- Apply this slant to all relevant content, including social media posts and keynote presentations as well as videos and podcast interviews.
- Share anecdotes that demonstrate how your unique approach delivers results.

Keep everyone on message
- Make sure your team understands your unique slant.
- Give your sales team specific examples of how to explain it.
- Check that your marketing materials clearly reflect it.

MIND SPARK QUESTIONS

What conventional wisdom in your field do you secretly think is completely wrong but have never publicly challenged?

If your biggest competitor were to steal one aspect of your approach tomorrow, which would hurt most to lose because it's so central to how you stand out?

What harsh truth about your industry are clients desperate for someone to finally acknowledge openly?

What strong point of view do you already hold that makes industry insiders uncomfortable when you share it but resonates deeply with your ideal clients?

EXERCISE
YOUR CONTRARIAN SLANT

Find your opposing view. Write down one common industry practice or belief you strongly disagree with and why.

Craft your slant statement. Complete this sentence: "Most people believe _____ , but here's a different way to look at it: _____ ."

Share it. Turn your statement into a social media post, the opening of your next speech or video, or a conversation starter with clients and prospects.

Your strongest opinions will make some people disagree. And that's good. A slant everyone agrees with isn't distinctive enough to stand out. Market leaders attract superfans and repel the wrong audience, using the exact right level of profitable polarization.

"It's more fun to be a pirate than to join the navy."

STEVE JOBS

3 FUTURE
YOUR VISION THAT LEADS

QUICK DEFINITION

If you don't paint a picture of where your industry is heading, someone else will. Your brand future is the tomorrow you see clearly today, and when you share it broadly, you give others a reason to follow you.

HOW TO THINK

People naturally follow those who can see around corners and advise on the risks and rewards that lie ahead. A compelling vision of the future doesn't just predict what's coming; it shows how you're already building it. This attracts the clients, team members, and partners who want to go with you on that adventure.

Name the next chapter
- What's changing in your target market that others haven't fully recognized?
- What will be different in two or three years that most people aren't preparing for?
- What outdated practices will fade away, and what will replace them?
- What are the risks posed by these changes?

Live your vision today
- Update your products and services to match where you say things are heading.
- Make small, visible changes that show you're committed to this direction.
- Share examples of how you're already implementing your vision.

Attract forward thinkers
- Talk about your vision in ways that resonate with clients who want to stay ahead.
- Highlight your future focus when recruiting team members.
- Connect with partners who share your outlook.

MIND SPARK QUESTIONS

What bold prediction about your industry would make your competitors uncomfortable if you made it public?

How are your clients, their needs, or their preferences changing?

What current industry practice do you see becoming obsolete first, and what specific evidence exists for that prediction?

If you were advising a client making a three-year strategic plan, what one emerging trend would you tell them they absolutely cannot ignore?

EXERCISE
YOUR INDUSTRY FUTURE SNAPSHOT

Define the shift. Complete this sentence:
"In five years, this industry will no longer _____ ; instead it will _____ ."

Share it. Post your statement on LinkedIn or your preferred platform, explaining your reasoning in simple terms.

Make it real. Choose one thing you can do this month that supports and spreads your bold vision of the future.

A strong future vision turns you into a magnet for high-value opportunities.

4 MEANING

UNLOCK DEEPER CONNECTIONS

QUICK DEFINITION

Your brand isn't just what you do; it's why it matters. Brand meaning creates the emotional connection that makes your audience truly care about your work.

HOW TO THINK

People don't just buy products and services. They invest in the **stories and feelings** those offerings create. When you tap into deeper meaning, you transform transactions into relationships. The strongest brands aren't just recognized or respected; they're **felt**.

Find your emotional core
- What emotion do you want people to experience with your brand? Trust? Aspiration? Excitement?
- Identify it so you can strike that chord consistently.
- What change are you helping people create in their lives or work?

Tell stories that show your impact
- Share real examples of how your work changed a client's situation.
- Talk about your own personal path and why the deeper purpose of your work matters to you.
- Highlight specific moments when your approach made a meaningful difference.

Weave meaning into everything
- Start videos, speeches, and webinars with why your topic matters, not just what you'll cover.
- Train your team to explain the purpose behind your work, not just the results.
- Look for ways to show your impact visually.

MIND SPARK QUESTIONS

Write down the last three times a client thanked you profusely or seemed genuinely moved by your work. What did they say to you? Not the "thanks for your help" stuff, but the real human reaction. Write down exactly what they said.

Now circle the **feeling** words they used. What did they express? Relief? Confidence? Freedom? Safety?

Then go deeper: What were they really thanking you for? Not the service, but what that service did for them as a person.

Now the tough part. When you strip away all the fancy features and benefits, what single emotional change does your work create?

"We help people feel _____."

EXERCISE
YOUR MEANINGFUL CONNECTION

Complete this sentence: "People don't just buy from us; they believe in _____ ."

Make it visible. Use this statement at the start of your next social media post, client presentation, or team meeting.

Check for alignment. Look at your recent marketing materials and ask:
- Does this clearly show our deeper purpose?
- Would someone understand why we care, not just what we sell?
- Does this connect emotionally or just list features, benefits, and outcomes?

The brands people love don't just solve problems; they stand for something that matters.

5 THINKING

OWN THE IDEAS THAT MATTER

QUICK DEFINITION

To achieve market eminence, you must own the thinking that shapes your industry. Market leaders don't follow trends; they define them. Your strategic thinking must be seen as the blueprint for the industry's future.

HOW TO THINK

When your ideas become the reference point for industry conversations, everything changes. People seek you out not just for what you sell but for how you think. This intellectual leadership creates opportunities that money can't buy.

Create deep, valuable content
- Regularly share substantial, thought-provoking content that truly helps your audience.
- Focus on solving real problems or explaining complex topics simply.
- Package your insights in formats people can easily use (trend reports, in-depth guides, visual frameworks).

Join important conversations
- Identify the places where industry decisions get made.
- Contribute thoughtful ideas rather than promotional messages.
- Connect with other experts to expand your influence.

Build your signature topics
- Choose two or three specific areas where you can provide unusual or surprising ideas.
- Consistently share fresh perspectives on these topics.
- Become the person who others associate with smart, forward-thinking insights.

MIND SPARK QUESTIONS

If you were asked to give a 15-minute TED Talk tomorrow about your industry's future, what provocative statement would you open with to immediately capture attention?

What intellectual territory in your field remains unclaimed that you could own if you consistently created content about it?

What complex concept do your clients struggle with that you could simplify better than anyone else?

If you had to write a short manifesto about how your industry is heading in the wrong direction, what would be the title and first line?

EXERCISE
THE BRAND THINKING CHALLENGE

Choose your territory. Pick one topic where your expertise can truly help others. Example: "Simplifying data security for small businesses."

Create something substantial. Develop a piece of content that shows your best thinking:

- A detailed guide solving a specific problem.
- A trend report with useful predictions.
- A framework that makes complex decisions easier.

Share it strategically. Instead of posting it randomly, be intentional:

- Send it directly to 10 key industry contacts.
- Offer it to a respected industry publication.
- Present it at an event where decision-makers gather.

"Thinking about thinking is the most important kind of thinking."

CATEGORY PIRATES

6 RESISTANCE

FIGHT WHAT'S WORTH FIGHTING FOR

QUICK DEFINITION

The most powerful personal and company brands don't just stand for something. They stand against something, making them sharper, bolder, and more magnetic. Taking a stand against outdated practices, persistent myths, or bad behaviors you refuse to tolerate takes courage and conviction, but it pays massive dividends.

HOW TO THINK

This one is hard. You'll need to face down fear: the fear of being skewered on social media, fear of the thought police coming after you, fear of looking like an idiot in public. Overcoming those fears is incredibly worthwhile because when you clearly oppose something that frustrates your clients, you become the refreshing alternative they've been searching for. Meaningful resistance creates natural differentiation. The best news: It also mobilizes an army of like-minded allies, champions, and supporters.

Name what's wrong
- What common practice in your industry actually hurts clients?
- What outdated approach do competitors cling to that you reject?
- What frustrates people about dealing with businesses like yours?

Share it loudly, publicly, and often
- Clearly explain in your content why you oppose this practice.
- Show examples of how it hurts people.
- Become the antidote to what's broken and present your alternative approach with confidence.

Make it part of your story
- Train your team to explain what you stand against and why, not just what you offer.
- Include your opposition in sales conversations as a key differentiator.
- Use your resistance as a screening tool for hiring and partnerships.

MIND SPARK QUESTIONS

What industry practice makes you genuinely angry when you see competitors using it with their clients?

If your top three competitors disappeared tomorrow, what harmful industry practice would likely disappear with them?

What's one thing your company privately refuses to do that you've never publicly taken a stand against?

What frustrating experience do your clients consistently mention having with other providers before finding you?

EXERCISE
YOUR "WE REJECT" STATEMENT

Find your opposition. Identify one industry practice you refuse to accept. Example: "We reject the idea that consulting must be complicated and expensive."

Craft your statement. Complete this sentence: "We reject _____, which is why we do _____ instead."

Amplify it. Include this statement in your:
- Website's About Us section.
- Sales conversations.
- Social media profiles.
- Next team meeting.

Resistance creates clarity about exactly who you are and who you're not. If no one hates your guts, no one truly loves you either.

7 GIFTS

LOVE THEM IN ADVANCE

QUICK DEFINITION

In a world of short attention spans, a brand gift is your ability to give immediate value while building long-term demand.

HOW TO THINK

People are bombarded daily with content that wastes their time. When you consistently deliver relevant value in every interaction, you stand out sharply. Giving people useful insights before they become clients creates trust that drives business growth.

Make every touchpoint count

- Review each way people interact with your firm. Is there real value every time?
- Whether it's a LinkedIn post, keynote, or sales call, ensure people walk away with something useful.
- Remove anything that takes time without giving something back.

Remove unnecessary barriers

- Simplify how people engage with your content and company.
- Use clear, jargon-free language.
- Eliminate friction and add surprise and delight everywhere possible (your agreements, invoices, proposals, client gifts, voicemail greeting).
- Make next steps obvious and easy to take.

Deliver results in advance

- Create tools, templates, or frameworks that people can use immediately.
- Offer insights and guidance that get results even before your prospects commit to working with you.
- Solve a small problem completely rather than a big problem partially.

MIND SPARK QUESTIONS

What's the one thing your clients consistently have to wait for that could be delivered immediately with minimal effort on your part?

When was the last time you were delighted by a company giving you value before asking for anything in return? What specific element could you adopt for your business?

If a prospect only had five minutes with you, what single piece of advice could you share that would create an immediate positive result for them?

What is one unnecessary step or barrier in your client-onboarding process that you could eliminate today to make your clients' lives easier?

Which of your competitors consistently deliver the most immediate value in their marketing? What specific tactics do they use that you're not currently employing?

EXERCISE
THE INSTANT GIFT AUDIT

Check your recent impact. Look at your last 10 pieces of content or conversations:
- Did people gain something useful right away?
- Would someone feel their time was well spent?
- Did you solve a real problem, even a small one?

Create quick wins. List three specific, practical insights you could share that:
- Take less than five minutes to understand.
- Can be implemented without buying anything.
- Deliver noticeable results quickly.

Measure what matters. Track how people respond:
- Which content gets the most engagement?
- What advice do people use and mention later?
- How does providing value first change your conversion rates?

The brands people love most don't just promise future benefits; they deliver real value with every interaction.

Make gifts a habit, not an occasional bonus.

8 CERTAINTY
CONVICTION THAT CONVERTS

QUICK DEFINITION

Brand certainty deepens trust in your authority. When you project confidence backed by proof, people feel secure following your guidance and buying your solutions.

HOW TO THINK

In a world full of empty promises, **certainty stands out**. When clients sense absolute confidence in your ability to deliver, they relax into trusting you. This trust accelerates decisions and builds lasting relationships that competitors can't easily break.

Eliminate uncertainty in your language
- Replace hesitant language ("we might" or "possibly") with clear, direct statements.
- Be specific about what clients can expect from working with you.
- Speak with clarity, confidence, and conviction about your products and services and in your advice and perspectives.

Show proof, not promises
- Share detailed case studies with specific numbers and outcomes.
- Use client stories that match the exact situation, goals, and challenges this specific prospect is facing.
- Include concrete "what to expect" metrics that prove your approach works.

Overdeliver on expectations
- Make your brand synonymous with rock-solid reliability, flawless execution, and consistent results.
- Follow through on every commitment, no matter how small.
- Create systems that ensure reliable, high-quality experiences for every client.

MIND SPARK QUESTIONS

What's one specific claim you make about your services that you can't currently back up with concrete numbers or client examples?

If you recorded your last three sales calls, what hesitant or uncertain phrases would you catch yourself using that might be undermining trust?

Which one of your competitors projects the most certainty in their marketing? What specific language or proof elements do they use that you could adopt authentically?

What's the single most impressive client result you've achieved that you're not prominently featuring in your sales materials, and why aren't you highlighting it?

If you had to guarantee one specific outcome to every new client (with money back if you don't deliver), what would you be confident enough to promise?

EXERCISE
YOUR CERTAINTY BLUEPRINT

Find your proof points. Identify three specific areas where you can be more concrete, for example:
- Replace "significant improvement" with exact percentage increases.
- Name specific clients who achieved specific results (with permission).
- Share the exact time frame in which results were achieved.

Update your materials. Add these specific proof points to your website case studies, sales presentations, and team training materials.

Check your language. Review your recent communications for uncertain phrases and replace them with something firmer, for example:
- "We will" instead of "we hope to."
- "We deliver" for "our goal is."
- "You will experience" for "you might see."

True certainty isn't arrogance. It's the quiet confidence that comes from your deep competence.

9 GRAVITY

BECOME A MARKET MAGNET

QUICK DEFINITION

Brand gravity is about becoming a magnet for clients, investors, and top talent. When you have it, you don't chase opportunities; they start chasing you.

HOW TO THINK

You're in the most powerful position in any market when you're **the one people want to work with**, not the one constantly pushing, pitching, and striving. True gravity transforms your business from hunting for clients to carefully selecting the best ones from those that come to you.

Own your specialty

- Choose one specific area where you can truly excel so that prospects, media, and partners associate you with it.
- Create consistently valuable content around this topic.
- Become the obvious answer when people have questions in this area.

Align with high-level peers

- Identify who already has the audience you want to reach.
- Find authentic ways to collaborate with other respected voices.
- Get seen alongside other market leaders to elevate your credibility and reflect your genuine value.

Turn demand into exclusivity

- The more sought-after you are, the more selective and expensive you can be.
- Communicate how you will change clients' future trajectory long-term.
- Set elite standards that position you as a reassuringly expensive investment, not arbitrarily overpriced.

MIND SPARK QUESTIONS

What specific client results could you highlight that would justify charging premium rates compared to competitors in your industry?

If you could only accept half your current clients tomorrow, what selection criteria would you use to choose the best ones for your business?

What concrete steps could you take in the next 30 days to position your services as a high-value investment rather than just another expense?

What language in your current marketing materials unintentionally signals "commodity" rather than the exclusive expertise that clients would consider themselves lucky to get access to?

What would change in your business if you approached every prospect conversation with the mindset that they need to qualify for your time, not the other way around?

EXERCISE
BUILD YOUR GRAVITY PLAN

Map your current reach. Write down the platforms where people already see and hear from you, such as:
- Industry publications.
- Social media channels.
- Professional networks.

Choose one growth target. Identify the one that's best for reaching more of your ideal audience:
- An industry publication or blog.
- A podcast that interviews people in your field.
- An event where you could speak.

Create your 90-day plan. For your chosen platform, plan specific steps:
- Month 1: What will you create or contribute?
- Month 2: How will you deepen your presence?
- Month 3: How will you turn visibility into real opportunities?

Gravity isn't built overnight. Stay consistent and focused, and it will happen faster than you think.

10 RISKS

SMART BETS THAT PAY OFF

QUICK DEFINITION

Not all brand risks are worth taking. Remember when Starbucks published a magazine? Probably not, because it failed quickly. The right risks separate market leaders from followers, while the wrong ones waste resources and confuse your audience.

HOW TO THINK

Taking smart risks can set you apart and create breakthrough opportunities. But random experiments often lead to **expensive distractions**. The key is knowing which risks align with your core strengths and which ones don't belong in your playbook.

Be bold, but strategic
- Challenge industry norms, experiment, and push boundaries, but not without thinking.
- Test ideas that align with your unique strengths.
- Look for gaps in the market that others have missed.

Avoid the "we should do that too" trap
- Just because competitors are doing something doesn't mean it makes sense for you.
- Question whether new trends actually fit your brand identity.
- Focus on what makes you different, not what makes you similar.

Test before you commit
- Before rolling out a bold initiative, gauge audience reaction with a test or smaller version.
- Gather honest feedback about what's working and what isn't.
- Own your mistakes and adjust quickly. If a brand risk fails, pivot fast and openly admit the misstep.

MIND SPARK QUESTIONS

What bold move have you been afraid to try that your competitors would hate to see you succeed with?

When was the last time you killed a "good idea" because it didn't truly fit who you are as a brand?

If you had to bet half your marketing budget on one risky but potentially game-changing approach, what would it be?

Think about your last failed initiative. Did it fail because the idea was wrong or because you weren't brave enough to fully commit to it?

EXERCISE
THE SMART RISK FILTER

Choose one opportunity. Identify a new initiative or risk you're considering, such as a new service line, a different marketing approach, or a potential collaboration.

Test against your core. Ask these questions:
- "Does this truly align with what we do best?"
- "Will this strengthen our brand identity or dilute it?"
- "Are we pursuing this because it fits us or because others are doing it?"

Design a small test. If the idea passes your core test:
- What's the smallest version you could try first?
- How will you measure if it's truly working?
- What clear results would make you expand or end the experiment?

Smart risk-taking means being bold where it matters while having the discipline to say no to distractions.

11 MYTHS

CHALLENGE THE BS

QUICK DEFINITION

Industry myths are beliefs or perceptions that seem true because they're widely accepted, but they're holding you, your clients, and your entire industry back. Dispelling these myths can create powerful new opportunities.

HOW TO THINK

When everyone believes the same thing, questioning those beliefs creates immediate differentiation. Challenging established "truths" captures attention and opens doors to market segments that others ignore. The most innovative brands often start by rejecting what "everyone knows."

Identify limiting beliefs

- What outdated beliefs or self-soothing delusions are limiting your potential, misleading your prospects, or otherwise holding back your whole industry?
- Which accepted practices frustrate your clients, team, or partners but persist anyway?
- What keeps certain types of clients underserved?

Take a bold stand

- Clearly explain why the common belief is wrong, incomplete, or factually misleading.
- Share evidence that challenges the accepted wisdom.
- Be vocal about the false ideas, half-truths, and misinformed concepts your brand rejects.
- Confidently present your alternative perspective as "uncommon sense."

Turn myths into opportunities

- Develop products or services based on your different viewpoint.
- Create content that educates people about the reality.
- Connect with the audiences that others neglect because of these myths.

MIND SPARK QUESTIONS

Which clients have you helped succeed by going against conventional industry wisdom that everyone else follows?

If you could erase one misleading belief from your clients' minds before they talk to you, what would make the biggest difference?

What solution are you uniquely positioned to offer because you reject an industry myth that your competitors still believe?

EXERCISE
MYTH-BUSTING 101

Spot the false beliefs. Write down three myths that dominate your industry. Example: "You need an enormous budget to get results with digital marketing."

Create your counterstatement. For each myth, write a clear challenge: "Small businesses can actually outperform bigger competitors by focusing on targeted digital strategies rather than broad campaigns."

Share your perspective. Use these counterstatements as the foundation for:
- Blog posts, videos, or social media content.
- Client conversations and presentations.
- Team training and company messaging.

When you dispel myths, you not only stand out, but you create the space to build something truly different.

12 FRIENDS

THE COMPANY YOUR BRAND KEEPS

QUICK DEFINITION

Your brand friends are the companies, influencers, and experts who can reinforce your credibility and amplify your message when you work together.

HOW TO THINK

No brand succeeds alone. The right partnerships can open doors to new audiences, strengthen your credibility, and create opportunities that would be impossible on your own. Smart collaborations accelerate growth by leveraging each partner's unique strengths.

Find the right matches
- Who already has the attention, respect, or business of the audience you want?
- Identify other experts whose values and approach align with yours but don't compete directly.
- Focus on quality partnerships rather than quantity of connections.

Start by giving value
- Support their content and promote their initiatives before asking for anything.
- Share insights or resources that would benefit their audience.
- Look for genuine ways to help them achieve their goals.

Create win-win collaborations
- Co-host events, podcasts, and industry panels. Co-create research, videos, or ebooks.
- Make it easy for partners to work with you by being prepared with assets, tools, and content they can use.
- Measure results together to build on successful partnerships.

MIND SPARK QUESTIONS

Who already has your dream audience's trust that you could partner with instead of compete against?

What company outside your industry has a brand style you admire and could join you for an unexpected but powerful collaboration?

Which potential partner would most surprise your competitors if you announced a joint project tomorrow?

What unique asset or insight do you have that would be genuinely valuable to a bigger brand's audience?

If you could only pursue one strategic partnership this year, which would help grow your visibility the most?

EXERCISE
BRAND FRIEND ACTIVATION

Create your friend list. Identify five companies or experts who align with your mission:
- Who already serves your ideal customers?
- Whose expertise complements yours without competing?
- Who shares your values but brings different strengths?

Make the first move. For each potential partner, plan a specific offer:
- A piece of content you could create together.
- An event you could co-host.
- A resource you could develop for their audience.

Start small and grow. Begin with a simple collaboration:
- Set clear goals for what both parties hope to achieve.
- Track results to measure the partnership's value.
- Use successful small projects to build toward bigger opportunities.

Focus on creating real value for your partner and their audience, not just what you can gain.

13 LENS
YOUR SIGNATURE WAY OF SEEING

QUICK DEFINITION

How do you see the world differently? Your brand lens is the unique framework through which you analyze problems, spot trends, and create solutions.

HOW TO THINK

Anyone can share information, but true market leaders provide a new way of seeing the world. When you offer a clear framework that helps people understand complex issues, they naturally turn to you for guidance.

Define your viewpoint
- What worldview, philosophy, or foundational approach do you have that shapes the way you see your industry?
- How do you approach problems differently from others?
- What insights have you gained that could help others see more clearly?

Create a branded method
- Package your perspective into a method or process.
- Give your approach a memorable name.
- Make it visual so that people can easily grasp and remember it.

Share your lens widely
- Teach your approach consistently across all platforms.
- Show how your method solves real problems.
- Invite others to apply your lens to their own challenges.

MIND SPARK QUESTIONS

What approach or method do you use that clients often say they've never seen before?

What visuals do you consistently draw on a napkin, your iPad, or a whiteboard when working with clients?

Which problem in your industry seems complex to others but looks simple through your unique perspective?

What consistent steps do you always take when tackling challenges that you've never thought to name or formalize before?

What's the one question you always ask that completely changes how people think about their situation?

EXERCISE
THE FRAMEWORK BUILDER

Identify your method. Choose one area where you consistently solve problems:
- What steps do you naturally follow?
- What questions do you always ask?
- What elements do you consider that others often miss?

Create your visual model. Organize these insights into a framework:
- Use five to seven clear components (steps, principles, or elements).
- Give it a simple, memorable name.
- Create a basic visual that shows how the parts connect.

Start teaching it. Choose three places to share your lens, for example:
- Create a presentation explaining each component.
- Write an article outlining your approach.
- Use it consistently in your speeches, videos, live streams, and sales conversations.

The more your audience understands and adopts your lens, the more you control the conversation.

BONUS TIP

Create an on-demand executive briefing that teaches your branded method or lens. Make it available on your website. See this example: www.doitmarketing.com/ceo-brand.

14 MANIFESTO

YOUR BOLD DECLARATION

QUICK DEFINITION

A brand manifesto is a loud, proud, and bold declaration of who you are, what you stand for, and why your market should follow you. It's your rallying cry for meaningful change, and ultimately it's one of the main drivers of your positioning and differentiation.

HOW TO THINK

When you clearly state what you believe and why it matters, you attract the right people and repel those who don't share your vision. Your manifesto becomes the foundation of everything you say and do.

Make it personal and powerful
- Write it from the heart, not like a corporate mission statement.
- Get personal. Rant, rave, wax, wane, compare, contrast, and have some fun with it.
- Humor wins buy-in and humanizes your message.

Declare your beliefs
- What's right with the world?
- What's wrong with the world?
- Don't just give us the how-to; tell us how to think about and prepare for what's coming next.

Make it public

Reference your manifesto in your conference keynotes, in social media content, on your website, and in your recruiting and onboarding process.

MIND SPARK QUESTIONS

What gets you fired up about your industry that you haven't had the courage to say publicly yet?

If you had to write a declaration that would make half your industry uncomfortable but deeply resonate with your ideal clients, what would it say?

What belief about your work feels so obvious to you that you're surprised others don't see it the same way?

If you could only share one passionate belief about your field with every potential client before they made their buying decision, what would it be?

EXERCISE
THE MANIFESTO BUILDER

Capture the building blocks of your manifesto. Use the following prompts:

- Write down 10 bullets under the heading "What I Know for Sure."
- Write down 10 opposites, using the format "It's not about X, it's really about Y."
- Write down 10 surprising or contrarian facts about your products, services, or industry.
- Write down 10 common myths and the 10 corresponding truths.

Remember, information is not enough. Clients hire you for your insights, opinions, biases, recommendations, values, and crazy ideas. Thus, it **pays** to be contrarian, counterintuitive, and compelling.

Once you've captured the building blocks, **refine them** with your team or favorite AI tool.

The most powerful manifestos aren't safe or predictable. They repel the wrong people as much as they attract the right ones.

BONUS TIP

Download three sample manifestos from the book bonus page at www.marketeminence.com.

15 MANTRAS

YOUR QUOTABILITY QUOTIENT

QUICK DEFINITION

A brand mantra is a one-line philosophy that defines how you think, act, and lead. When you develop a set of these mantras, they become short codes that serve as key differentiators in building your market eminence.

HOW TO THINK

In a world of information overload, short and powerful statements cut through the noise. When you consistently use meaningful mantras, they become associated with you and help others remember and share your ideas. These signature phrases become verbal logos that represent your entire approach.

Keep them brief and memorable
- Limit each mantra to three to ten words to maximize impact.
- Use simple, everyday language that's easy to remember.
- Make sure it captures a genuine belief so that it's not just a catchy slogan.

Use them consistently
- Reinforce and repeat them in meetings, sales calls, and your online content.
- Include them in team discussions and decision-making.
- Use them as touchstones when facing challenging situations.

Build your collection
- Start with one or two core mantras that capture your essence.
- As your company grows, add new mantras without compromising the nature of the whole collection.
- Notice which ones resonate most with your audience.

MIND SPARK QUESTIONS

What phrase do you find yourself saying over and over that clients now repeat back to you?

What single statement captures your approach so perfectly that you wish it were tattooed on every client's mind?

If you could only give one five-word piece of advice to someone in your field, what would pack the most wisdom?

What's the simplest truth about your industry that most people overcomplicate?

What short phrase would you want to be remembered for long after you've stopped working in this field?

EXERCISE
YOUR MANTRA COLLECTION

Capture your sayings. Create two simple lists:
- Ten short phrases (three to ten words) that express your core beliefs.
- Ten "you-isms" (phrases people quote back to you).

Examples:
- "Simple always wins."
- "Start with what it means, not what it does."
- "Fix the system, not the symptoms."

Test their power. For each potential mantra, ask:
- Does it clearly express an important belief?
- Is it easy to remember and repeat?
- Does it feel authentic to you and your brand?

Start using them. Choose your best mantras and:
- Include them in your next presentation.
- Use them to set team priorities.
- Add them to your social media profiles or website.

BONUS TIP

Here are some examples of mantras my firm has developed that we share with consulting clients and speaking audiences all the time:

- Action eliminates fear.
- If they don't have your fee, they're not your prospect.
- Relentless focus on MMA (money-making activities).
- Money loves speed and time kills deals.
- Helping before pitching.
- Serving before selling.
- Sales is about relevance, value, and relationship.
- No one accomplishes anything great alone.
- If you don't risk turning some people off, you'll never turn anybody on.

FORTUNE COOKIE MANTRAS

To stimulate your creative juices, here's a fun selection of real fortune-cookie fortunes I've collected over the years:

- Many receive advice; only the wise profit by it.
- A career really is a quest.
- Trust your intuition. The universe is guiding your life.
- To be fulfilled, you need work that is compatible with many aspects of your personality.
- Doubt is often the beginning of wisdom.
- Dare to change so you can be yourself.
- Things are more likely today than they ever have been before.
- Don't be afraid to swim against the tide.
- A conclusion is the place where you got tired of thinking.
- Success means adapting to new rules.
- You are confident, intelligent, caring, and attractive.

The most powerful mantras are magic words that build differentiation, recognition, and trust.

16 BREAKAGE
STRATEGIC REINVENTION

QUICK DEFINITION

It's important to know when and how to reinvent yourself. Sometimes, breaking your brand to rebuild stronger is the key to long-term success. This is true for both your personal brand and your company brand.

HOW TO THINK

Markets evolve, customer needs shift, and staying relevant sometimes requires more than small adjustments. The strongest brands don't wait for crises to force change. They proactively reinvent themselves while they're still successful.

Strategic breakage creates space for new growth: Paper company Kimberly-Clark sold its paper mills to focus on the consumer business of Huggies and Kleenex. IBM stopped selling computers and became a global consulting firm. What do you need to break?

Spot what's holding you back
- If a brand message, strategy, or service no longer feels relevant or doesn't resonate the way it used to, break it.
- Look for declining impact or results.
- Be honest about where you're falling behind competitors.

Act before you have to
- Make changes while you're still strong, not when you're struggling.
- Plan your reinvention rather than reacting to problems.
- Set a timeline for transformation before the market forces it.

Lead through the transition
- Clearly explain the reasons for change to customers and team members.
- Highlight what will stay the same alongside what will change.
- Communicate the change confidently by fully owning the shift, which will help bring your audience along.

MIND SPARK QUESTIONS

What part of your brand worked three years ago but doesn't match who you are today?

If you could shed one outdated aspect of your business without fear of backlash, what would you gladly leave behind?

Which competitor's bold pivot secretly made you think, "We should have done that first"?

What change have you been avoiding because it feels too risky, even though you know it's necessary?

EXERCISE
THE BREAK-OR-KEEP FRAMEWORK

Identify change candidates. List three things that might need to break given market conditions, client needs, competitive pressure, or technological advances. Examples:
- A positioning that no longer differentiates you.
- A delivery approach that feels outdated.
- A product, service, or message that doesn't align with your bold new trajectory.

Protect your foundation. Determine what must stay:
- Only break things to strengthen your future position.
- Breakage doesn't mean throwing everything away.

Create your transition. Map out a plan that balances boldness and strategy:
- Set specific goals for what the breakage/reinvention should achieve.
- Create a timeline with milestones and stages.
- Plan how you'll communicate the changes to different audiences.

Breaking aspects of your brand isn't about erasing your history but about creating space for your next chapter.

17 LANGUAGE

WORDS THAT SET YOU APART

QUICK DEFINITION

The specific words you choose (and avoid) have a powerful impact on how your brand is perceived. Your language should be distinctive, consistent, and immediately recognizable as uniquely yours.

HOW TO THINK

Generic language creates generic brands. When everyone in your industry uses the same words and phrases, nothing stands out. **Crafting a unique language** for your brand creates immediate differentiation and helps position you as a leader rather than just another option.

Develop your signature terms
- Create specific phrases that capture your unique approach.
- Name your methodologies, processes, or frameworks.
- Use words that reflect your brand's personality and values.

Establish an "always say / never say" guide
- Make a list of powerful words that align with your brand.
- Remove weak, generic, or overused words from your communications.
- Set standards for tone, style, and level of formality.

Ensure consistent usage
- Train your team to use your brand language naturally.
- Review your marketing materials for language alignment.
- Check for small nuances in vocabulary, tone, and style and update as needed.

MIND SPARK QUESTIONS

What industry jargon do you secretly hate that you still use in your marketing materials?

If you had to rename your core service or product with a term no competitor could use, what would capture its essence?

Which words consistently appear in your competitors' materials that you could deliberately avoid?

What's one concept central to your approach that deserves its own unique term rather than a generic description?

If clients were asked to identify phrases you use that no one else does, what would they say is distinctly you?

EXERCISE
THE BRAND LEXICON

Root out weak, generic words. List five common phrases you currently use that sound like all your competitors.

Create stronger alternatives. Craft bolder, sharper, more distinct language that is unique to your deep specialization, skill set, or proprietary methods.

Implement the changes. Update your key materials to reflect your revised brand language:
- Revise your website and social media descriptions.
- Update your elevator pitch and sales talking points.
- Refresh how you introduce yourself and your firm.

Thoughtful, distinctive language creates immediate impressions about what you do, how it's different, and why it's attention-worthy.

18 LEGENDS

STORIES WORTH RETELLING

QUICK DEFINITION

Legendary brands aren't just known. They have iconic stories that get retold and passed down. These are leadership stories, brand stories, customer stories, sales stories, and culture stories.

HOW TO THINK

Facts and features don't stick in people's minds, but when you share compelling stories, people connect emotionally and remember you. The right stories create a legacy that builds trust, loyalty, and recognition that lasts far longer than any marketing campaign.

Craft your origin story

- Make it compelling, memorable, and deeply connected to your firm's manifesto points and beliefs.
- Highlight the problem you set out to solve.
- Connect your beginning to your current purpose.

Document client transformations

- Collect specific stories of how clients experience your generosity, kindness, or going above and beyond.
- Include details that show your unique approach.
- Focus on emotional impact, not just practical results.

Share your challenges

- Be honest about obstacles you've overcome.
- Recall stories of grit and tenacity to show how difficulties shaped your character.
- Demonstrate resilience that builds confidence in your brand.

MIND SPARK QUESTIONS

Which client success story would make the perfect opening for a talk about your unique approach?

What personal challenge shaped your business philosophy that you rarely share with clients?

If your company history were made into a movie, what would be the pivotal scene that changes everything?

What unexpected connection or coincidence in your business evolution feels almost too perfect to be true but really happened?

EXERCISE
THE ICONIC STORY

Identify your most powerful narrative. Write a one-paragraph version of your brand's most compelling story:

- What challenges did you overcome?
- What unexpected insight changed everything?
- What customer moment showed the true impact of your work?

Share it strategically. Use this story in:

- Your next presentation, webinar, or client meeting.
- A social post or video that explains your purpose.
- Conversations with your team about your company's mission.

Refine based on response. Pay attention to how people react:

- Which parts of the story do people mention later?
- What questions does it spark?
- How does it affect people's understanding of your brand?

The best legends and stories are NOT about you. Focus on your clients, your team, your partners, and your impact.

19 FRICTION
TO PROTECT AND TO SERVE

QUICK DEFINITION

Not all friction is bad. Some tension forces clarity, differentiation, and stronger positioning. The right amount of friction can create market dominance. Luxury boutiques post well-dressed guards at the doors specifically to allow the right people in and keep the wrong people out. This friction protects the brand and serves their best clients, who want to feel elite, valued, and invited to an experience designed exclusively for them.

HOW TO THINK

Brands that try to please everyone end up connecting with no one. Strategic friction (intentional barriers or strong positions) can filter out the wrong clients while deeply attracting the right ones. When used wisely, friction creates clarity about who you are and who you serve best.

Embrace the right kind of friction
- A little controversy or contrast makes you stand out.
- Be willing to zig where everyone else zags.
- Use tension to highlight what makes your approach different.

Use friction as a sales asset
- Be specific about who isn't your ideal client.
- Create processes that naturally filter out poor-fit prospects.
- Focus on serving the right people extremely well, not everyone adequately.

Create an emotional hook
- Challenge your audience to think and feel differently than your competitors do (or don't!) with theirs.
- Ask questions that make people reconsider their assumptions or even challenge them head-on.
- Create content that sparks meaningful conversation.

MIND SPARK QUESTIONS

If you had to create an application process for new clients, what three questions would reveal whether they're right for you?

What's one step you could add to your sales process that would drive away price-shoppers but attract serious clients?

Which competitor tries to be everything to everyone that you could position yourself against by being proudly specialized?

What warning label would you put on your services that would scare away the wrong clients but intrigue the right ones?

EXERCISE
THE FRICTION TEST

Find your friction point. Identify one area where your brand creates tension. Examples:
- A requirement before people can work with you.
- A strong position that differs from industry norms.
- A process that asks more of your clients than competitors do.

Assess its value. Determine whether this friction:
- Attracts your ideal clients and repels poor fits.
- Demonstrates your quality and expertise.
- Creates confusion or unnecessary barriers.

Refine your approach. Based on your assessment:
- Strengthen productive friction that enhances your positioning.
- Remove barriers that simply frustrate good prospects.
- Clearly explain the purpose behind intentional friction.

When friction is purposeful, it can transform from an obstacle into a powerful filtering and sorting tool.

20 MOMENTUM

BECOME AN UNSTOPPABLE FORCE

QUICK DEFINITION

Market eminence isn't just about occasional spikes of attention; it's about sustaining momentum over time. Controlling your brand's energy ensures you remain consistently visible and influential.

HOW TO THINK

Many personal and company brands follow a boom-and-bust cycle: They make a big splash and then disappear. This pattern forces them to rebuild attention each time they need it. When you maintain steady momentum, you create deep and lasting marketplace respect, recognition, and reputation.

Balance your visibility
- Create a consistent cadence of content and appearances.
- Avoid exhausting sprints followed by complete silence.
- Maintain a baseline of activity that keeps you visible between major moments.

Connect your growth channels
- Ensure your different platforms and activities support each other.
- Use speaking engagements, podcasts, and webinars to fuel content creation.
- Offer to exchange and distribute content from a select group of trusted partners, as they do the same for you.

Create anticipation cycles
- Plan launches and announcements strategically throughout the year.
- Always have something coming next that your audience can look forward to.
- Use each milestone to build energy toward the next one.

MIND SPARK QUESTIONS

If you had to create a content calendar that required zero heroic effort but kept you consistently visible, what three simple activities would it focus on?

If your brand suddenly went silent for 30 days, what would your audience miss most about your presence?

What "coming soon" element could you tease right now that would make your audience eagerly anticipate your next move?

Which competitor maintains the most consistent presence in your industry, and what one habit or pattern could you steal from their playbook?

EXERCISE
THE MOMENTUM METER

Check your current momentum using these indicators:
- How visible have you been over the past 30 days?
- What's the cadence of your content?
- Does your audience know what's coming next?

Plan your energy peaks. Map out major moments for the next 90 days:
- One significant content piece or event each month.
- Promotional activities to build anticipation before each peak.
- Follow-up content that extends the impact after each peak.

Fill the valleys. Create consistent engagement to become omnipresent to the right audiences:
- Weekly content that maintains visibility.
- Regular touchpoints to engage your audience.
- Ongoing online and offline activities that keep your brand present, valuable, and helpful.

Action leads to traction. Traction leads to momentum. Momentum leads to results.

21 SPEED

MOVE FAST AND KEEP MOVING

QUICK DEFINITION

Have you embraced the power of moving faster? Speed wins. Brands that execute quickly, respond in real time, and get ahead of trends dominate the market. Want proof? Check out my friend Jay Baer's terrific book, *The Time to Win: How to Exceed Your Customers' Need for Speed*.

HOW TO THINK

The window for capitalizing on opportunities is often measured in days, not months. When you build speed into your brand operations, you create a competitive advantage that's difficult to match.

Cut the decision-making lag

- Eliminate unnecessary approval layers that slow implementation.
- Empower your team to make decisions without constant oversight.
- Create clear guidelines that enable faster action.

Go before you're 100 percent ready

- Ship when your offering is viable, not when it's perfect.
- Get real-world feedback instead of endless internal reviews.
- Remember that being first often matters more than being flawless.

Build a culture of agility

- Build processes designed for speed and adaptation.
- Gather and apply feedback continuously.
- Encourage, celebrate, and reward fast action, fast feedback, and fast iteration.

MIND SPARK QUESTIONS

If your industry suddenly moved twice as fast, which of your current processes would immediately break down?

What opportunity did you miss in the last year because your response time wasn't quick enough to capitalize on it?

Which competitor consistently beats you to market, and what one system could you change today to match their velocity?

What "good enough" version of your next big idea could you launch within 72 hours if you were forced to?

EXERCISE
THE NEED FOR SPEED

Break decision paralysis. Identify one decision you've been overthinking:
- Make the call today, even without perfect information.
- Document your reasoning but don't delay further.
- Start implementing immediately.

Set speed deadlines. Choose one delayed project and:
- Complete a viable version within 48 hours.
- Focus only on essential elements.
- Launch to a small group for immediate feedback.

Build a speed culture. With your team, establish new norms:
- Create a "ship fast, refine later" mentality.
- Celebrate quick implementation over perfect execution.
- Share examples of when speed created advantages.

The market rarely punishes you for moving too quickly, but it almost always punishes you for moving too slowly.

BONUS TIP

Download the Market Eminence Roadmap to help you navigate from invisible to irresistible in four stages. Get it from the book bonus page at: www.marketeminence.com.

MARKET IN

PART THREE

EMINENCE

ACTION

22

THE MARKET EMINENCE MODEL

All the strategizing, positioning, and differentiation are now in place. You're ready to act.

There are three primary components to activate and amplify your market eminence: Speaking, Publishing, and Podcasting.

1. SPEAKING
TRANSFORM FROM A BEST-KEPT SECRET TO VISIBLE WISDOM

Speaking is one of the fastest ways to earn recognition. It allows you to connect directly with key audiences, demonstrate expertise, and **build trust in a powerful, personal way**.

The three critical focus areas you must get right are:

Compelling topics. Your speaking success starts with topics that matter to your audience:

- **Address urgent gaps:** Speak about specific problems, challenges, headaches, and risks.
- **Offer fresh perspectives:** Share new ways to think about old problems, backed by data, stories, or case studies.
- **Deliver uncommon wisdom:** Every talk should leave attendees with actionable takeaways they can immediately apply as well as new perspectives and new ways of thinking.

Contrarian messaging. Stand out by challenging conventional wisdom:

- **Debunk industry myths:** Highlight common misconceptions and explain why they're holding your audiences back.
- **Share bold predictions:** Be willing to take a stand on what's coming next in your industry.
- **Present unique solutions:** Offer approaches that no one else is talking about but are grounded in your expertise. Reframe old problems with new contexts and insights.

Targeted audiences. Speaking to the right people is just as important as what you say:

- **Identify ideal venues:** Focus on conferences, trade shows, and webinars where your target stakeholders are present.
- **Collaborate with organizers:** Build relationships with event planners to position yourself as the perfect fit for their audience.
- **Engage attendees before and after:** Use speaking opportunities to generate leads and nurture relationships through carefully designed follow-up strategies.

2. PUBLISHING
EVOLVE FROM JUST ANOTHER VENDOR TO CREDIBLE AUTHORITY

Publishing is key for building market eminence at scale. By sharing your ideas through books, blogs, articles, and social media, you command attention and respect in the minds of your audience.

Our most successful clients implement the following:

Callout content. Great publishing starts with calling out the specific problems or challenges your audience faces:

- **Define their pain points:** Write about the exact problems they have or results they want.
- **Speak their language:** Use the exact language your audience uses to describe their issues.
- **Create targeted content:** Address specific roles, industries, or circumstances to make your message feel personal. Make them say, "I feel you were talking directly to **me**."

Shifting beliefs. Your content should challenge assumptions and shift perspectives:

- **Address myths and truths:** Write articles or book chapters that help readers unlearn outdated ideas. Help them see gaps, contradictions, and self-soothing delusions.

- **Offer a new lens:** Encourage your audience to think differently about their challenges and opportunities. The more differentiated, opinionated, and contrarian, the better.

- **Focus on root causes:** Explain why certain strategies work and others don't, adding depth to your message.

Consistent activation. Consistency is critical to staying relevant:

- **Activate weekly:** Don't post and run. Once a week, deploy your content in specific marketing, sales, and growth initiatives. Send to prospects, clients, partners, investors, or the media.

- **Repurpose vigorously:** Chunk up and chunk down. Compile blogs, articles, and newsletters into books or ebooks, or turn book chapters into articles, videos, or social media posts.

- **Engage with feedback:** Respond to comments and conversations to build deeper connections with your readers. Tag and reply, then engage privately via DM if appropriate.

3. PODCASTING
MOVE FROM AN ISOLATED AUDIENCE TO EXPONENTIAL REACH

Podcast guesting offers an unparalleled opportunity to connect with audiences and expand your reach, especially when you bring your sharply differentiated talking points, a refreshing and authentic voice, and organic conversion strategies. Once guesting starts to get results, consider if hosting a podcast makes sense for you.

Power up your podcasting results these ways:

Narrow niche. Focus your podcast guesting efforts on dominating a specific vertical or industry niche:

- **Research hosts and shows:** Identify podcasts that align with your expertise and target audience. Find shows that guests in your niche have appeared on to multiply your results.

- **Tailor your message:** Customize your content for each audience to increase relevance and impact. Show the host you've done your homework on their exact audience.
- **Stay consistent:** Appear regularly on niche podcasts to build momentum and recognition over time. Showcase your podcast appearances on your website for evergreen promotion.

Scalable attraction. Expand your audience through deliberate strategies:

- **Borrow audiences:** Appear as a guest on podcasts that cater to your exact target audience.
- **Leverage collaborations:** Partner with hosts or guests to share content across multiple channels. Use leapfrog strategies so that each podcast leads to three or four more.
- **Amplify content:** Repurpose podcast episodes into blogs, articles, video snippets, executive summaries, process visuals, social posts, or newsletter content.

Reliable conversion. Use podcast guesting as a system to turn listeners into leads:

- **Create a call-to-action:** Encourage listeners to download a free resource, watch an on-demand training or demo, or book a call.
- **Prepare belief-busting talking points:** Challenge the audience's existing assumptions to build curiosity and engagement. Be unlike any other guest they've ever had on their show.
- **Track conversions:** Use analytics to measure how effectively your podcast appearances are generating leads. Use different offers that appeal to cold, warm, and hot leads.

THE THREE PILLARS IN ACTION

When speaking, publishing, and podcasting come together, they create a powerful synergy that propels you toward market eminence:

- **Speaking** builds visibility, so you're regularly seen by key stakeholders.
- **Publishing** builds credibility, ensuring your voice stands out in a crowded market.
- **Podcasting** builds shareability, amplifying your message and expanding your audience.

CONCLUSION

YOUR BRAND LIVES IN YOU!

Look, you didn't need another book on branding filled with fluff, clichés, or generic advice that could apply equally to a car company or a TikTok fashion influencer.

You're here because you lead an expert services firm and want to escape "best-kept secret" status once and for all. You've earned it because you've built something valuable, smart, and different. And now it's time the market **knows it**.

As you've seen, this book isn't just about "personal branding." It is about **market domination**.

Visibility.
Credibility.
Power.
Status.
Respect.

It is about **you** using the full spectrum of your gifts (your thinking, your voice, your values, your vision) to turn your company into a powerful magnet and yourself into an unstoppable force.

You now know what separates the **obscure** from the **outstanding**, the **replaceable** from the **irreplaceable**, and the **overlooked** from the **overbooked**.

Let's recap what you've built in these pages:

- A brand with **gravity**, where partners, clients, customers, investors, the media, and top talent come to you.
- A voice with **clarity**: Say goodbye to muddled messaging, same-o lame-o positioning, and "meh" content that is easily ignored.
- A platform with **precision**: speaking, publishing, and podcasting that put you everywhere your market is already paying attention.
- A presence with **edge**: Your brand now stands **for** something, stands **against** other things, and gets the right people excited with productive polarization.
- A business with a vibrant **identity**: boldness, energy, intelligence, and a movement that people want to invest in, advocate for, and get others to join.

You've architected the foundations of your own market eminence.

Now, the only question is: Will you **implement** it, or will this become just another smart book that sits on your shelf?

If you're serious, then now is the time to act.

First, do the work to build out your strategy, point of view, and true differentiation using the ideas you just read about.

Then start to operationalize your market eminence in the real world:

- **Speak** like a category creator.
- **Publish** like your brand depends on it (because it does).
- **Podcast** like you're already the number one voice in your industry.

Your next level starts now. Go build a brand that dominates, resonates, and lasts. I'm in your corner.

Let's do it!

REACH OUT TO ME ANY TIME

Email: david@doitmarketing.com
Web: www.doitmarketing.com
Book bonuses: www.marketeminence.com

TAKE THE NEXT STEP

The Market Eminence Roadmap call is a zero-cost, 30-minute private session for CEOs, founders, and expert services firm owners designed to:

- **Assess** your current visibility and authority.
- **Identify** gaps in your speaking, publishing, and podcasting efforts.
- **Create** a customized action plan to elevate your personal brand and company brand.
- **Determine** if and how we can be of further help to you and your organization.

There are a limited number of spots each week. Apply for your call right here: **www.doitmarketing.com/call**.

ONE FAVOR BEFORE YOU GO...

If *Market Eminence* made you think differently...

If it gave you more clarity, stronger firepower, and new tools to elevate your brand...

If you underlined, highlighted, or dog-eared even one idea...

Would you be wonderful enough to write a 2-sentence, 5-star positive, poetic online review?

Reviews are the lifeblood of every book. They help new readers discover the ideas inside. They help the book earn trust and credibility. And they help authors like me continue to create work that matters. Your voice makes a difference.

Go to your favorite online bookstore, find *Market Eminence*, and click "Write a Review." Tell others what you found valuable, what changed for you, or what you'd say to someone thinking of reading it.

I appreciate you!

DAVID

P.S. Thank you for your time, your support, and your generosity. I don't take any of it for granted.

ABOUT THE AUTHOR

David Newman is a Certified Speaking Professional (CSP), keynote speaker, and host of the podcast *The Selling Show*, which is ranked in the top 1 percent globally and has over 500 episodes. He works with founders, CEOs, and experts who want to play bigger, grow faster, and become a category of one.

David's previous books are *Do It! Selling*, *Do It! Speaking*, and *Do It! Marketing* (an international bestseller translated into six languages).

He has been featured and quoted in *The New York Times*, *Investor's Business Daily*, *Forbes*, MSN, StartupNation, FastCompany.com, Sales & Marketing Management, Selling Power, CNBC, and *Entrepreneur* magazine.

David has presented over 600 keynotes, seminars, and strategic work sessions since 1992. In addition to the mid-market CEOs and professional services firms he works with today, his past clients and audiences include forty-four of the Fortune 500, such as IBM, Microsoft, Oracle, Accenture, KPMG, PNC Bank, Merrill Lynch, and American Express.

WANT MORE?

Get free companion trainings, templates, and tools at **www.marketeminence.com** and a ton of other cool resources at **www.doitmarketing.com**.

www.ingramcontent.com/pod-product-compliance
Lightning Source LLC
Chambersburg PA
CBHW060356080526
44583CB00012B/334